THE TOXIC PEOPLE

Signs and ways to deal with them in a relationship

JEFFERY GAD

Table of contents

YOU OFTEN FEEL USED BY THEM
EVEN THOUGH YOU KNOW THEY AREN'T GOOD FOR YOU, YOU STAY WITH THEM ANYWAY
THEY ARE LIKE A DRUG
SOWING SEEDS IS HER FAVORITE PASTIME

CHAPTER FIVE

THEY ARE NOT ENCOURAGING
IT'S ALL ABOUT THEM
YOU RARELY AGREE, BUT YOU ARE AFRAID TO SPEAK YOUR MIND
THEY'RE NOT THERE WHEN YOU NEED THEM
WHEN THEY CALL, PART YOU DOESN'T WANT TO ANSWER
THEY BRING OUT THE WORST IN YOU

CHAPTER SIX

THEY NEVER APOLOGIZE
THEY LIE...A LOT
THEY GET GRUMPY IF YOU DON'T PAY ATTENTION 24/7
THEY LIKE TO JUDGE
THEY HAVE BIG PROBLEMS WITH THEIR EGO
THEY NEVER CONSISTENT
THEY TALK ABOUT YOU
THEY ARE ABUSIVE

CHAPTER SEVEN

YOU ALWAYS FEEL LIKE YOU HAVE TO PROVE YOURSELF
THEY ARE SKILLED MANIPULATORS
YOU OFTEN FEEL YOU HAVE TO PROTECT YOURSELF
THEY USE WORDS AGAINST YOU

INTRODUCTION

The most harmful toxin you touch, literally makes everything around you sick or kills everything as a result. Even if it feels good at first, it sucks you in and does more damage than you can imagine. A toxic person is like a drug. They feel really good and excited when they meet for the first time. Over time, your trust in them will destroy you to the core. The biggest problem with toxic people is that they don't realize they're hurting you. We all come across toxic people in our lives. We'd be surprised if we've lived this long without encountering a toxic person. They don't necessarily have to be partners. Even family members, co-workers, and co-workers can show signs of being a toxic person. Even if you know precisely who is toxic in your life, you don't always know how to label it. There are always people, and it never works. In the end, you get hurt when she's trying everything to get her to love and accept you. But recognizing the signs can help you understand who you're dealing with and how to get out of this situation. Being around toxic people can be inevitable, but knowing the signs can help you understand how to deal with them. Toxic people work by taking advantage of you. Like crabs, they seek to destroy and conquer all. Don't give in to them or fall into their traps. The best way to keep from

falling into their hands is to
see who they are before you
make contact. You should
heed these warning signs from
toxic people.

CHAPTER ONE

They are never happy

Toxic people feel frustrated no matter what they are doing or who they are with. If you are with someone who sees nothing but despair, things will probably not go well for you. Like a constant obstacle, it's hard to maintain peace and happiness when you're constantly finding an anti-silver lining in every situation.

Worse, there is nothing you can do to make her happy. You make a great effort to appease them. In the end, they have nothing in return but misery.

Toxic people make themselves look and feel better by destroying the people around them. They must always have a "goal" to focus on. If they're talking about someone to you, they must be talking about you to someone else. It's only a matter of time before everything changes for you.

They only feel good when they put other people down.

A very possessive person feels in control only when someone is around them. To do this, they must divide your friends and conquer all the good things in your life. They want to have you all to themselves and make sure you break up with everyone else in your life.

Toxic people make you want to get involved. Do you know

someone who makes you talk negatively about someone or something and when you walk away from them you feel ugly and mean? They don't challenge you to be the best, they make sure you're the worst. You should look for another place in

CHAPTER TWO

Toxic people are people you fear because you can't beat them. They are the ones you never speak your mind about. You certainly don't disagree with them. If so, you risk becoming their next target. The problem is that if you don't confront them at some point, you will become their target, whether you like it or not. The best way to deal with a toxic person is to walk away quietly and, if possible, not wave their wings.

They take out an entire room

A toxic personality draws life out of a room or office. Like cancer, they overcome everything that's going on and make them feel nauseous. You will hear what is wrong. You are usually the one standing in a corner and bending someone's ears about how bad life is, how bad someone is, or how bad their life is. There is nothing good for a toxic person.

Toxic people's goal is to get the attention of those around them, but for obvious reasons, they are not very well-liked and usually cannot sustain friendships for long. When people realize who they are, they try to keep their distance. Most toxic people aren't just toxic to you. They leave a trail of unhealthy friendships in their tracks.

They are very possessive

They are happy only when they are in control of

someone. To do this, you need to hold the person tightly. As an It person, I don't like it when I have to share my BFF with someone else, so I do everything I can to make sure there is no competition.

They don't Filter Words

Their parents never taught them, "If you can't say something nice, don't say anything. "Say something positive and they will surely find a way to tear everything apart.

CHAPTER THREE

Toxic people never get what they want. They usually go for what they don't have. Always trying to get more, you give up the most valuable things such as friendships. He relentlessly manipulates his environment to get what he wants and what others have.

They always have to get mad at someone. In some cases, the target does not need to do anything. If they are jealous or jealous, they are not beyond making things up. Their goal is to turn their backs on anyone who disagrees and work hard behind the scenes to do so.

One day you will be their best friend and the next day they will stop caring about you. They only want you by their side if you serve a purpose. It makes you feel worthless, and that's their plan.

Always know your friendship is on the edge where just one bad move can put you out. If so, all your secrets, and some

made-up secrets, will be
scattered all over the place.

CHAPTER FOUR

They make you feel bad after you leave them

When you leave, you feel like a used-car salesman—for doing things you're not proud of, interfering in things you probably don't want to do, and putting up with things you really don't agree with. I know.

You never feel like you get a word in edgewise

I'm raising my voice. You never feel like you can talk because it's all about her.

Most of the time you don't
want this because I spend
countless hours telling you
what to do.

You often feel used by them

I know that spending time
with them is just skin deep.
They don't care what you have
to say, so you always feel like
you've been used to the end by
some means.

*Even though you know they
aren't good for you, you stay with
them anyway*

Either because you are
charismatic or just because

you are scared. You maintain friendships with them.

They are like a drug

When they're nice to you, it feels great like you've finally reached the "real" them. The real you soothe you and keep you riding. If you always want to get their attention and be nice, chase the next high.

Sowing seeds is her favorite pastime

They usually come straight out and don't say what they mean. Passive aggression and seeding are the basis of all of them. They leave it up to you to fill in the blanks, so if anything goes wrong they just point a finger.

CHAPTER FIVE

They are not encouraging

If you have a problem, don't go to them. Always there to point out the obvious "shit" of the situation, they never have a word of encouragement or a way to lift your spirits when you really need it.

It's all about them

Friendship is a one-way street. They exist only as tools to make you feel good about yourself or to get what you want.

Toxic people don't want to listen to you. In fact, they scare you into going against the grain. You always know the backlash of saying no or going against what they want, so you always do what they want or just nod.

Very selfish and one-sided when it comes to toxic people. You'd better be there when they need you, but you can only get their attention.

You try to avoid them because you know in your heart that they don't do you any good. When her contact shows up, you will find yourself nervous and not having a constructive conversation.

The worst part about being in a toxic relationship or dating a toxic person is that they have an uncanny ability to bring out the absolute worst in you. It's because they react badly to other people's actions or speak ill of others. When you're around her, you're not who you want or know you should be.

CHAPTER SIX
They never apologize

Toxic people never apologize...why should they? It's never her fault. If someone never apologizes for their actions, they will never consider their actions a mistake.

They refuse to admit their mistakes, apologize right away when you voice their opinion and always try to turn things around and make it their problem, not theirs.

If you think someone is toxic, look at how honest they are. Toxic people usually lie all the time and take responsibility and care. The worst thing is that you can actually see the situation and hear them lie. They don't care, they're not shameful, and they certainly can't be trusted.

They get grumpy if you don't pay attention 24/7

Maybe you had a bad day today and need someone to talk to. Instead of listening to you, they always need your attention. Otherwise, they'll either get more dramatic and emotional, or they'll move away from you and look for someone else.

Being close makes you feel like you are under a microscope. Quickly evaluate each step. They're the first to criticize you, whether it's how you dress, your love life, your career, or your body. Unfortunately, it won't help you. Instead, her voice gets

34

stuck in your head and pulls you back in. They thrive in abstinence.

They have big problems with their ego

For toxic people, think the whole world revolves around them. They hang out with you because you make them feel big. Look, they think they're the best thing to walk this earth. They are smarter, better looking, and more talented than you. Wrong, that's what they think.

If you're looking for one of the most obvious traits of toxic people, it's that they don't really know what they're thinking. One day they will tell you one thing and the next day they will say something completely different. Their opinions change depending on who they are with and what they want. Their dishonesty is not what you want around you.

You may have something to say, but they won't let you say it. Instead, they shut you down and talk about you. That way, they can make sure they get the spotlight and not say things that make you look smarter, funnier, or better than them.

They are abusive

We are not necessarily talking about physical abuse, but they are certainly emotionally and mentally abusive. Stay away from them

CHAPTER SEVEN

You always feel like you have to prove yourself

They seem like your friends, but they always force you to prove yourself. Even if you do everything for her, you feel like you're not a good friend. It shows that you are sacrificing your own needs for the needs of others and must cut them down.

They are skilled manipulators

You may not have realized it until now, but they are advanced manipulators. Their overall goal is to get you to do something that they want, to make their life better, not yours. If you're with a toxic person, it's not an equal relationship.

If they are disinterested in the topic or not listening to you, they are manipulating the situation. Instead, the focus is on determining exactly how you talk about the discussion, what you say, your tone, and your choice of words.

They use words against you

There are many words that are neither toxic nor negative. Toxic people, however, can use harmless language in their tone of voice. They never openly say how they feel. For example, if you didn't make dinner like you said, instead of asking why you didn't make dinner, they would say, "You didn't seem to do much today.

They are terrible at listening

It can be difficult to actively listen to someone when it's a topic you're not particularly

40

interested in. But if it's your friend, family member, or coworker, you want to actively listen and show support...but toxic people aren't interested in listening at all. They quickly change the subject.

CHAPTER EIGHT

They play the victim card

Victim cards are the only cards toxic people can play because they always work for them. Why should they change now? They appear innocent and helpless while blaming others for their problems. In reality, they made mistakes and have to take responsibility for them.

They blame you for their misfortune

We all have bad days and inadvertently take them up on

the people we love most. In such cases, we acknowledge our wrongdoing and apologize. But that doesn't always happen when someone is in a bad mood. They need to take responsibility and work on their feelings.

You need to defend your decision

Whenever I make decisions about them, big or small, I always feel the need to defend my decisions. You guess your emotions and intelligence. Did you make the right choice? If you don't feel like you're around them, it's a sign that a toxic person is playing with your mind.

Sarcasm can be really funny. However, excessive sarcasm is insulting and can really hurt people's feelings. But for toxic people, sarcasm is based on anger and distrust, so it is one of their most powerful weapons.

Being around her is like walking on eggshells. Warm

and friendly one day, grumpy
and upset the next. You never
know what you'll get, and
you'll always feel alert. Your
need to please them only
makes it worse.

CHAPTER NINE

We all have good days and bad days, but that doesn't mean your friends, partners, or family members have to have negative emotions. Just because someone feels bad doesn't mean the other person doesn't feel bad either. But one of the most obvious signs of a toxic person is his malice, which makes everyone around him suffer as much as he does.

We all have personal boundaries that others must respect. People usually quickly figure out where your limits are based on talking to you and their experiences. Toxic people don't respect your boundaries. Your boundaries are there to define and protect who you are. If they can't respect it, that's a red flag.

When you're depressed, they're uplifted

They don't party with you when you're doing well in

life...but when you're feeling down, they shine. They are volatile and jealous, so their good news is never good. But your bad news, it's good news for her. They may tap you on the shoulder to calm you down, but their eyes light up with joy!

CHAPTER TEN
Conclusion

When it becomes clear that you have a toxic person, or multiple people, in your life, it's time to distance yourself from that person. If they are family members or co-workers, you may not be able to completely cut them out of your life, but you can set your own personal boundaries and stick to them. It's best to cut them out of your life and not feel bad about it. Sometimes you have to put yourself first.

But if that's not possible, limit the amount of time you spend together. Remind yourself regularly that this person is toxic and their emotions are due to it. You need to stay true to yourself and avoid falling into their poison traps. Don't waste your time building relationships with toxic people who don't want the best for you and from you. It is to remove the toxins from the area and start over.

www.ingramcontent.com/pod-product-compliance
Lightning Source LLC
Chambersburg PA
CBHW061316140726
47998CB00006B/2421